And The Winer Is...

Fabulous Women Get Their Just Rewards

Illustrations & Text

by

Jim Smith

copyright 2018
jimsmithart.net

"America
is always
Great."

— Glenda
Jackson
6/10/18

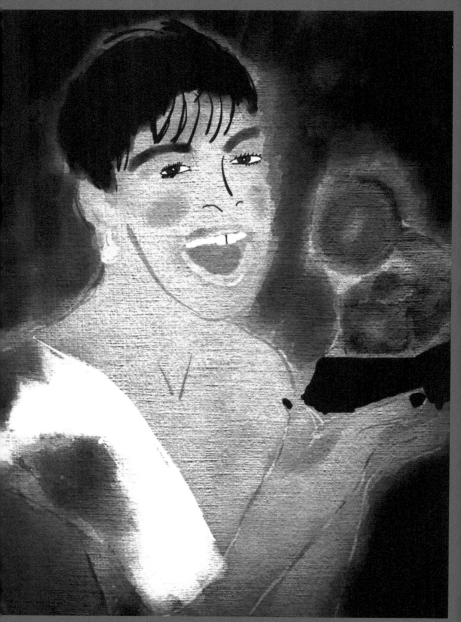

24

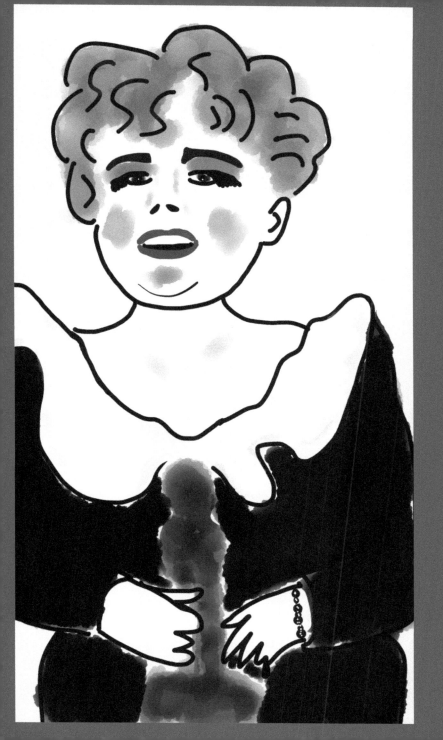

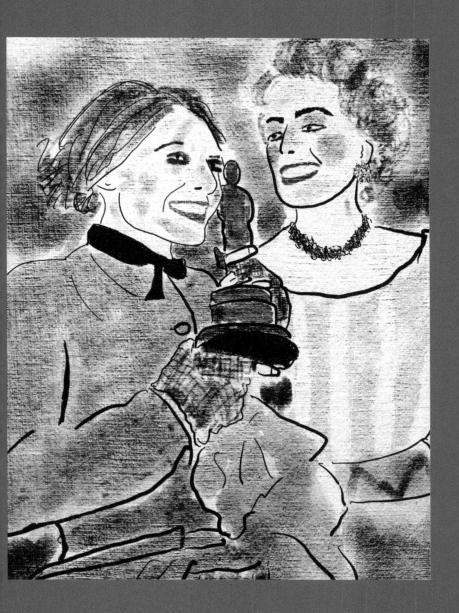

Index of Illustrations

Page 2-3, Barbra Streisand receives an Oscar as Best Actress for her film debut in *Funny Girl* on April 14, 1969. A few years earlier, on September 12, 1965, she won an Emmy for Outstanding Individual Achievement in Entertainment for her first television special *My Name is Barbra.*

Page 4, Agnes Moorehead, a four time Oscar nominee, wins an Emmy in 1967 for her supporting work in an episode of *The Wild Wild West.*

Page 5, Kathy Bates wins her second Emmy in 2014 for *American Horror Story Coven.*

Page 6, Glenda Jackson, age 82, wins the 2018 Best Actress in a Play Tony Award for *Edward Albee's Three Tall Women* and uses her speech to extol the virtues of America

Page 7, Helen Mirren wins the 2015 Best Actress in a Play Tony for playing Elizabeth ll in *The Audience.* Eight years earlier she'd won an Oscar for playing the same character in *The Queen.*

Page 8, Natalie Cole with her 2009 Grammy for *Still Unforgettable,* one of nine she won during her career.

Page 9. Ella Fitzgerald with one of her 12 competitive Grammys. (Lifetime achievement and Hall of Fame mentions put her over 20 wins)

Page 10, Angelica Huston takes home the Best Supporting Actress Oscar in 1986 for *Prizzi's Honor*, making her a third generation winner.

Page 11, For her role as dog trainer Muriel Prichett, Geena Davis wins the Supporting Actress Oscar in *The Accidental Tourist* (1988)

Page 12, Audrey Hepburn, as a princess in hiding in *Roman Holiday*, is named Best Actress at the Oscars in 1954.

Page 13, Audrey Hepburn poses backstage with Julie Andrews, who had just won the Best Actress Oscar for *Mary Poppins* in 1965. Audrey failed to win a nomination for her performance as Eliza Doolittle in *My Fair Lady*, a role Julie had originated on stage.

Page 14, Maggie Smith receives her Best Actress Oscar for *The Prime of Miss Jean Brodie* from Lauren Bacall backstage at the Tony Awards. The Oscars ceremony had taken place a week earlier on April 7, 1970, but Maggie was in London performing in a play. She flew to New York for one day to present a special Tony to Alfred Lunt and Lynn Fontanne, and picked up her Oscar.

Page 15, Susan Sarandon takes home the Best Actress Oscar on her 5th nomination for 1995's *Dead Man Walking* , becoming the first actress to win for playing a nun.

Page 16--17, Costume designer Edith Head with one of her eight Oscars; she holds the record for most wins by a woman in any category.

Page 18-19 , Enigmatic Italian performer Anna Magnani with her Best Actress Oscar for *The Rose Tattoo.* She did not attend the ceremony, but there are no shortage of photos of her posing with the statue later.

Page 20, Carly Simon with her Best Song Oscar for "Let the River Run" from 1988's *Working Girl.*

Page 21, Marion Cotillard wins the Best Actress Oscar in 2008 for her riveting portrayal of Edith Piaf in *La Vie en rose.*

Page 22-23, Stockard Channing wins the Best Actress in a Play Tony Award for the drama *A Day in the Death of Joe Egg* in 1985; three years later her *Joe Egg* co-star Joanna Gleason takes home the same award in the Musical category for playing the Baker's Wife in *Into The Woods.*

Page 24-25, Carol Channing wins the Best Actress in a Musical Tony Award for *Hello, Dolly!* and 53 years later Bette Midler wins the same award for a revival of the same show. Bette had some choice words for the play-off music, as she was determined to finish her speech.

Page 26, Eileen Brennan wins an Emmy in 1981 for her work as a cranky army captain in the TV version of *Private Benjamin;* just months earlier she'd been nominated for an Oscar for playing the same role on film.

Page 27, Two-time Tony winner Sandy Dennis poses with a trophy at the 1968 ceremony. She also won an Oscar during her career.

Page 28-29, Patty Duke, age 16, wins the Best Supporting actress Oscar for *The Miracle Worker* in 1963; six years later Ruth Gordon, age 72, wins in the same category for *Rosemary's Baby.* At the time of their wins, they were, respectively, the youngest and oldest competitive acting winners.

Page 30-31, Three-time nominee Angela Lansbury accepts an honorary Oscar in 2013, and two-time nominee Gena Rowlands is likewise honored in 2015.

Page 32, Ingrid Bergman wins the first of her three Oscars on March 15, 1945 for *Gaslight*.

Page 33, Shelley Winters wins her second Best Supporting Actress Oscar in 1966 for *A Patch of Blue*. Winters donated her first Oscar, for *The Diary of Anne Frank*, to the Ann Frank Museum in Amsterdam.

Page 34, Joan Crawford poses with her *Mildred Pierce* Oscar and a bottle of Pepsi in front of her portrait.

Page 35, Anne Bancroft did not attend the ceremony when she was named Best Actress for *The Miracle Worker* because she was appearing in a play in New York. In a stunt designed to piss off Bette Davis, Joan Crawford famously picked up the award on Bancroft's behalf. A month later Joan presented it to poor Anne, still in her tattered costume and dirty makeup as Brecht's *Mother Courage* on the stage of Broadway's Martin Beck theatre.

Page 36, Shirley MacLaine and Barbra Streisand at the Golden Globes in 1984. Shirley won a Best Actress in a Drama award for *Terms of Endearment*, while Barbra won two trophies for *Yentl*, one for producing and one for directing--the first woman so honored.

Page 37, Oprah Winfrey gives a stirring rallying call of a speech at the 2018 Golden Globes as she accepts the Cecil B. DeMille Award.

Jim Smith is pop culture enthusiast and illustrator. He lives in Philadelphia with his Jack Russell Terrier Buster.

CPSIA information can be obtained
at www.ICGtesting.com
Printed in the USA
LVHW07s0504210818
587606LV00014B/79/P